"Reading the last outstanding poem by Meridel LeSueur, one feels that she unfurls to death in the same way she embraced life, hers and that of others, in a 'communal interaction,' 'communal participation,' 'communal society'—key words in all her works—a powerful legacy, a liberating possibility."

Laura Coltelli, author of Le radici della memoria. Meridel LeSueur e il radicalismo americano degli Anni Trenta *and translator of LeSueur's works into Italian, professor, University of Pisa*

"As one of Meridel's publishers, I know firsthand the strength of her will. She named her book *Ripening*, and she rejected the cover we prepared, saying she was not a 'crone.' We were obedient, feeling blessed by her grand presence. And so I am not surprised to learn that she was writing even to the moment of her death."

Florence Howe, founding publisher of The Feminist Press *at CUNY, author of* A Life in Motion: A Memoir

"We should not be surprised to hear in Meridel's last words echoes of all her words that came before, as she traces consciousness outward from the body through the forces of the land to the collective people, charged with memory must speak. And yet these ancient words remain new and funny and profound

Julia Allen, professor emerita, English Department, Sonoma State Uni

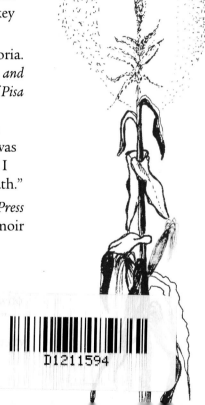

D1211594

This with my
last breath

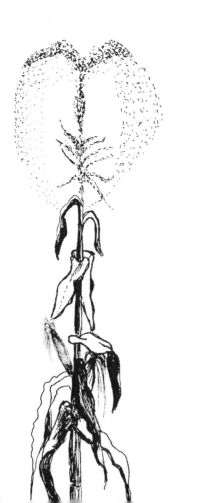

This with my last breath

Meridel LeSueur

Meridel LeSueur

Illustrations by Deborah LeSueur

Copy and Managing Editors: Deborah LeSueur, Lincoln Bergman, Jocelyn Tilsen, and Barbara Tilsen
Designers: Kimberly Nightingale and Daniel Tilsen
Proofreading assistance: Gayla Ellis, Kevin FitzPatrick, Jeannie Piekos, and Sally Heuer
Illustrator: Deborah LeSueur, originally appearing in *Rites of Ancient Ripening* by Meridel LeSueur

"Rites of Ancient Ripening" appeared in *Corn Village,* Stanton & Lee, 1970; in *Rites of Ancient Ripening,* Vanilla Press, 1975; in *Rites of Ancient Ripening,* David Tilsen and Meridel LeSueur, 1982; and in *Ripening,* Feminist Press, 1990. All rights reserved.

ISBN: 978-0-935697-12-4
First Printing – limited edition

Cover printed on 100 percent recycled content French Speckletone, produced with hydroelectric power.

Pages printed on 100 percent PCW recycled content Neenah Environment. Printed in the USA by Smart Set, Inc., Minneapolis, Minnesota

Published 2012 by Midwest Villages & Voices
P.O. Box 7034
Minneapolis, MN 55407

www.meridellesueur.org

Contents

Acknowledgments   ix
Foreword   xi

first breath

Introducing Meridel   5

deep breath

Remembrance   11

Rites of Ancient Ripening   13

last breath

Reflection   25

This with my last breath   29

Books by Meridel LeSueur   37

Acknowledgments

This project began as a kernel of an idea several years ago. The question of when we would be ready to send the last words of Meridel LeSueur out into the world has been on our minds since her death in 1996. She had something significant to say, and while we mourned her passing and cherished her work, we honored the privacy of the family while asking the question: when shall we present this work to the wider community?

Even though Rachel Tilsen, Meridel's oldest daughter, passed away in 1998, she was also very much on our minds and central to our planning and thinking as we created this book. We thank her for her love and dedication to the written word, her family, and community.

A special thank you must go to Kimberly Nightingale and Daniel Tilsen for their generous partnership in the inspired design of this book and for providing technical expertise. We greatly appreciate consultations by Ellen Lawson Design on the cover. Thank you to Phil Kasian and Kevin Brown for their invaluable advice in the production of this book. We are deeply grateful to Gayla Ellis, Kevin FitzPatrick, Jeannie Piekos, and Sally Heuer for their proofreading assistance and publishing expertise.

We thank Midwest Villages & Voices for supporting this project. Rachel and Meridel were two of its founding members and gave generously of their time and energy to this small press. We are pleased to collaborate with MV&V to bring the voice of this much-loved and greatly missed Midwestern writer to readers once again.

Consultations with David Tilsen, Miranda Bergman, and others were of invaluable assistance to us.

We appreciate the support of everyone around us, which allowed us to spend many hours in planning meetings and conference calls so we could present this work to you.

Deborah, Lincoln, Jocelyn, and Barbara

Foreword

From first to last, Meridel LeSueur's writing has been an inspiration for many generations, a living breath flowing from and through people's real experiences. She had an amazing ability to write directly from the center, the heart, the very essence, touching on the deepest truths. Her immense love, respect, and belief in the power of the people and the power of the word was ever-present in her work. She was a chronicler, a witness, a defender of people's lives and struggles. Throughout the years, Meridel regularly wrote in her journals; this was part of her discipline and her process as a writer. Much of her writing began in her journals as a kernel, a seed, a beginning, an exploration: a first breath.

To celebrate her 112th birthday, we present two of Meridel's writings that share her creative gifts in especially moving ways. We designed this book with three sections and set each page with an image of corn—a recurring symbol in Meridel's prose and poetry. Corn is a significant metaphor in her work with its communal female roots—ancient tiny grass seeds changed through time by indigenous women's ingenuity to nourish the children and the future. Our book begins with the section "first breath" introducing Meridel and describing her life. In the section "deep breath," we share her seminal poem about aging and death written circa 1970, "Rites of Ancient Ripening." This is one of her

most beloved poems; it reflects the profound ways she creates, weaving evocative words, earthy and inspired, redefining our perspectives.

In the final section, "last breath," we share the last thing she wrote—a poem, really more of a final journal entry—about the process of dying. She wrote this while she was dying. We have titled the poem, "This with my last breath," which inspired the title of this book. As the last writing breath of our mother, our grandmother, we feel it is time to send it into the world for all to breathe in and share together.

Deborah LeSueur, Lincoln Bergman, Jocelyn Tilsen, David Tilsen, and Barbara Tilsen

first breath

Introducing Meridel

"The people are a story that never ends,
a river that winds and falls and gleams erect in many dawns;
lost in deep gulleys, it turns to dust, rushes in the spring freshet,
emerges to the sea. The people are a story that is a long incessant
coming alive from the earth in better wheat, Percherons,
babies, and engines, persistent and inevitable.
The people always know that some of the grain will be good,
some of the crop will be saved, some will return and
bear the strength of the kernel, that from the bloodiest year
some survive to outfox the frost."

Meridel LeSueur, *North Star Country* (1945)

Meridel LeSueur's poetry, short stories, and novels are a beloved part of the cultural and political fabric of our times. She was one of the great literary and communal voices of the twentieth century, which her long life spanned. In describing her own roots, Meridel wrote, "I was born at the beginning of the swiftest and bloodiest century at Murray, Iowa, in a white square puritan house in the corn belt, of two physically beautiful people who had come west through

the Indian and the Lincoln country, creating the new race of the Americas by enormous and rugged and gay matings with the Dutch, the Indian, the Irish; being preachers, abolitionists, agrarians, radical lawyers on the Lincoln, Illinois, circuit. Dissenters and democrats and radicals through five generations."

Meridel was born on February 22, 1900, and she died in Hudson, Wisconsin, on November 14, 1996. As a child she lived in Iowa, Kansas, Oklahoma, Texas, and Minnesota. She believed in giving voice to people's struggles. She said she learned early to write down what they were saying, hiding behind water troughs in the streets, under tables at home, listening. Listening to the tales of the lives of the people, her writings were grounded in these grassroots, salt-of-the-earth stories and experiences of working people, the poor, the disenfranchised, the dispossessed. She strove to make history a living, moving entity in our lives. She often said that words should heat you, make you rise up out of your chair and move!

She led a colorful and vibrant life. As a young woman, she studied physical culture and drama in Chicago and New York City, and she plied her talent in the silent movies in California as a stunt woman. As a young activist, she lived for a time in Emma Goldman's commune in New York City. Throughout her life, she was part of the great social and political movements of her time. Her writing encompasses proletarian novels, widely anthologized short stories, partisan reportage, children's books, personal journals, and powerful feminist poetry. Her early works, in addition to revealing the depth of her working-class consciousness, also focus on the struggles of women, and particularly poor women, those sterilized without their consent in so-called mental hospitals, those on the breadlines, those whose lives and oppression more traditional left-wing ideologues did not comprehend. Her children's books find heroes and sheroes in US history and are especially noteworthy for their non-racist depiction of Native American peoples and cultures. Meridel believed her writing could be a bridge making connections across many different cultures. The diverse communities that identify with and celebrate her work are a moving testament to the depth and power of her writing.

This book from a radical writer, a worker in words, a poet and feminist far ahead of—yet totally in tune with—her times, once again brings us the voice of our grandmother Meridel—a voice of revolutionary wisdom and indomitable resistance. As she said, "Survival is a form of resistance."

Meridel's life and writings testify to the profoundly democratic idea that positive social change always bubbles up—and sometimes erupts—from below. With Marx she would agree that to be radical means to go to the root of things— and at the root of things are the people themselves. She would enthusiastically greet the new movements rising today.

It is our fervent hope that this publication of Meridel's last writing before her death will join with her many other works that survive to "outfox the frost."

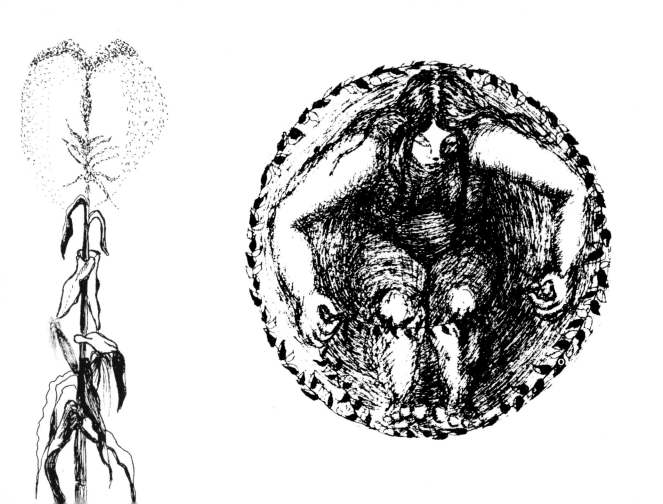

deep breath

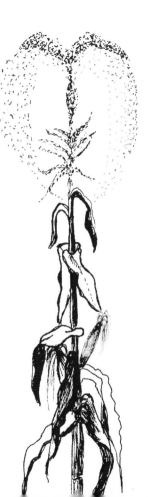

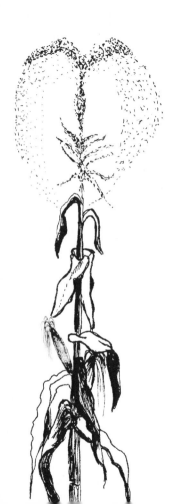

Remembrance

This poem, first published in 1970, represents Meridel in her prime. While she had always written poetry, the resurgence of the women's movement inspired and was inspired by her new poetic work. Although she would live another quarter of a century, her own aging, or ripening, now becomes a central theme, as does, naturally, death—"Toward the shadow of the great earth let me fall..." This poem and a number of other poems also find deep solace and sustenance in Native American spirituality, in the worldwide movements for radical change and against imperial war. Through it all sing visions of the relationship of death to life, that death is not an ending but a transformation—"corn died to bread/woman to child/deer to the hunters." Through it all are children and grandchildren—her ripening and death embodied in the generation to come. This poem's title also became the title of a book of Meridel's poetry celebrating sisterhood and global solidarity, illustrated by her daughter Deborah. Several of the drawings also grace this book.

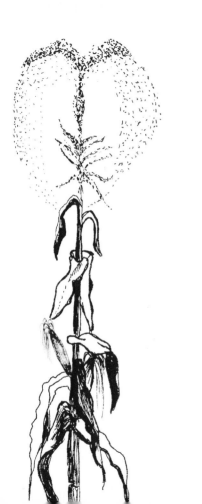

Rites of Ancient Ripening

I am luminous with age

In my lap I hold the valley.

I see on the horizon what has been taken

What is gone   lies prone   fleshless.

In my breast I hold the middle valley

The corn kernels cry to me in the fields

                    Take us home.

Like corn I cry in the last sunset

Gleam like plums.

                    My bones shine in fever

Smoked with the fires of age.

Herbal, I contain the final juice,

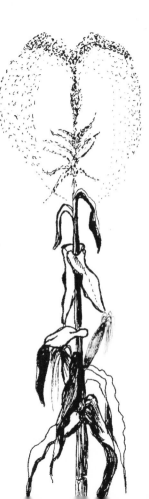

Shadow, I crouch in the ash
    never breaking to fire.
Winter iron bough
    unseen my buds,
Hanging close I live in the beloved bone
Speaking in the marrow
    alive in green memory.
The light was brighter then.
Now spiders creep at my eyes' edge.
I peek between my fingers
    at my fathers' dust.
The old stones have been taken away
    there is no path.

The fathering fields are gone.

The wind is stronger than it used to be.

My stone feet far below me grip the dust.

I run and crouch in corners with thin dogs.

I tie myself to the children like a kite.

I fall and burst beneath the sacred human tree.

Release my seed and let me fall.

Toward the shadow of the great earth

                        let me fall.

Without child or man

                  I turn   I fall.

Into shadows,

            the dancers are gone.

My salted pelt stirs at the final warmth
Pound me death

             stretch and tan me death
Hang me up, ancestral shield

             against the dark.
Burn and bright and take me quick.
Pod and light me into dark.

Are those flies or bats or mother eagles?
I shrink   I cringe
Trees tilt upon me like young men.
The bowl I made I cannot lift.
All is running past me.
The earth tilts and turns over me.

I am shrinking

   and lean against the warm walls of old summers.

With knees and chin I grip the dark

Swim out the shores of night in old meadows.

Remember   buffalo hunts

Great hunters returning

Councils of the fathers to be fed

Round sacred fires.

The faces of profound deer who

                gave themselves for food.

We faced the east the golden pollened

             sacrifice of brothers.

The little seeds of my children

            with faces of mothers and fathers

Fold in my flesh

        in future summers.

My body a canoe turning to stone

Moves among the bursting flowers of memory

Through the meadows of flowers and food,

I float and wave to my grandchildren in the

Tepis of many fires

        In the winter of the many slain

I hear the moaning.

I ground my corn daily

In my pestle many children

Summer grasses in my daughters

Strength and fathers in my sons

All was ground in the bodies bowl
corn died to bread
woman to child
deer to the hunters.
Sires of our people
Wombs of mothering night
Guardian mothers of the corn
Hill borne torrents of the plains
Sing all grinding songs
of healing herbs
Many tasselled summers
Flower in my old bones
Now.

Ceremonials of water and fire
Lodge me in the deep earth
   grind my harvested seed.
The rites of ancient ripening
Make my flesh plume
And summer winds stir in my smoked bowl.
Do not look for me till I return
          rot of greater summers
Struck from fire and dark,
Mother struck to future child.

Unbud me now

Unfurl me now

Flesh and fire

      burn

          requicken

             Death.

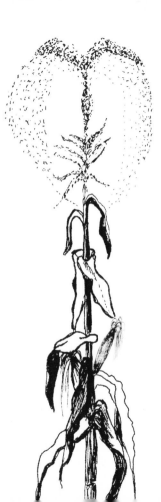

last breath

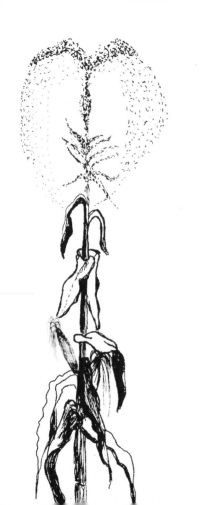

Reflection

Meridel wrote most of her life. She would say to us that to learn to be a writer, the most important thing to do is *to write*—to write something every day and work hard to communicate. She kept a journal from the time she was a teenager until she died. Her one hundred and thirty-three volumes of journals (from 1918–1991) are now at the Minnesota Historical Society, and they are a treasure.

Her published and unpublished work often began with the seeds of ideas, images, notes, and passages that she explored in her journals. She wrote about what she knew. Her writing grew directly from what she saw, heard, felt, and thought. She had the ability to record and report what she witnessed and observed, bringing these insights into her soaring poetry and prose. She evoked a personal and at the same time global understanding in her readers. She wrote poetry, novels, short stories, reportage, articles, and collections of works that defied categorization and genre pigeonholing. She was always writing!

Given this, in one sense, it's not surprising that when she was dying she was still writing. In another sense, however, it is astonishing. People talk about "famous last words," but rarely, if ever, does one hear about these being in written form. Meridel's daughter, Rachel Tilsen, was given the handwritten pages that were in bed with Meridel, on and next to her body, when she died. The words

of her final communication were not a polished completed poem, but rather free-flowing poetry in its initial journal form—rough, raw, and truly remarkable. Rachel—our sister, mother, aunt—led the work in putting this poem together. The text was at times difficult to decipher, but Rachel was more familiar than anyone with Meridel's handwriting, her imagery, her view of the world. Rachel had collaborated with and assisted Meridel on many writing projects throughout the years.

We call this poem "This with my last breath." It is extraordinary that Meridel used her reportage skills to record her final hours. Her ultimate words lead us into the experience of her dying. How striking her comparison of death to adolescence, how powerful her sense of "star built memory." How amazing that, at the very end of her life, she writes these words with her last breath.

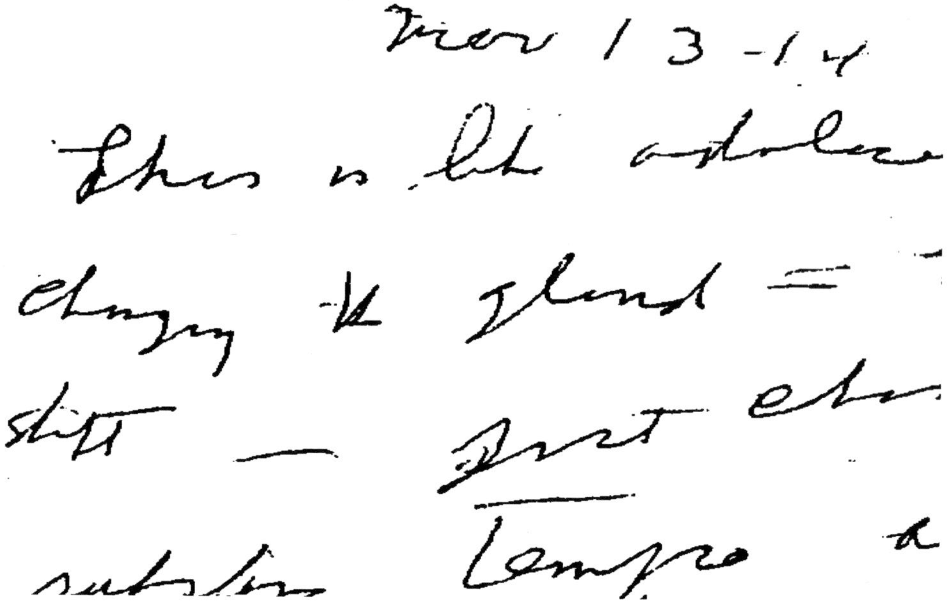

Excerpt from Meridel's handwritten pages, found with her when she died

This with my last breath

November — Thanksgiving

Nov. 13–14

This is like adolescence—all your body is
changing...the glands...the center glandular
shift...fast changes.
substance tempo another kind of sleep...
my reality seems different...I am a stranger to
myself...where are these alien feelings coming
from?

 O come to me...I am entertaining
some other person and nothing is familiar to me.

 It's not sleep...I am simply gone...

entirely gone from memory of the body and also

as if some dramatic character has

fallen from you and left you amazed alone

without your personality. Yes

you have died...that traditional person

and all her memories and took on alien

memories.

   It is strange you are taking

on a new personality...

a stranger...alienated...unfamiliar.

   I write differently...

   Then I seem to be gone

My body inhibits...immobile...

an empty house. I am sitting here as no one

absolutely no one. The wind blowing
into your valves and caves and habitat.

   Then another tide sweeps on all
the fire and identity of a powerful woman
of entire circulation. All the floods sing and
breaking new force and tide
and no need to do anything.

   We've taken off our persona and
removed a dress to make a study of bones.

   The death of the decorative person
comes back. Call back the naked and the reality.
We're shedding...what chickens do to
shed your feathers. Molt. Change your
reality.

But this shedding of all your
costume and personature is most amazing...
a certain clothing of personalities falls
away leaving you naked...bare.

　　Death of a shallow person.
Return to depth.
Death
Who is that with you?

　　　　It is one big movement...bring
the heart the blood flow in her river...
new return. In a movement from many
keening coming.

　　He comes now the night is ripening.
Yes. All up and down the great cottonwoods.

30 million died...

Trees of opulence.

September 1996

Girl   Girl

Behind being woman

Broken in the fragment of a stolen

nation...psychic notion. In the Indian world...

Indian earth a people on the earth.

Sound and resonance of earth...memory

Mind and flesh. Human mind flesh...

Carrying the print. Racial memory. Speak.

Communal culture   speak

O speak.   O speak.   O speak.

Liken centuries to give the dream and

the people.

New Crop

New Pace.

Mind and dream. The racial memory...build the body and mind the memory the song.

What is there to be given. Like insanity the pall of the directed...the ghostly.

It builds. The death builds.

The flesh is charged. Memory is present.

It is a substance. Slow down.

Slow fragments print with the body.

...a certain expectation. Star built memory.

It is slow.

What is real.

What builds.

What grows form.

What is fantastic...created.

What is real.

Books by Meridel LeSueur

Annunciation. Los Angeles: Platen Press, 1935.

Chanticleer of Wilderness Road. New York: Alfred A. Knopf, 1951; Duluth: Holy Cow! Press, 1990.

Conquistadores. New York: Franklin Watts, 1973.

Corn Village. Sauk City, WI: Stanton & Lee, 1970.

The Crusaders. New York: Blue Heron Press, 1955; St. Paul: Minnesota Historical Society, 1984.

The Dread Road. Albuquerque: West End Press, 1991.

The Girl. Albuquerque: West End Press, 1978, 2006.

Harvest. Albuquerque: West End Press, 1977.

Harvest Song. Albuquerque: West End Press, 1990.

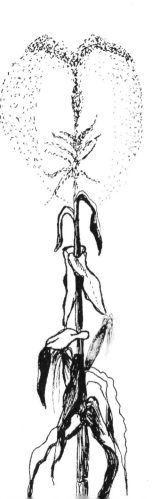

I Hear Men Talking. Albuquerque: West End Press, 1984.

I Speak from the Shuck. Browerville, MN: Oxhead Press, 1992.

Little Brother of the Wilderness: The Story of Johnny Appleseed. New York: Alfred A. Knopf, 1947; Duluth: Holy Cow! Press, 1987.

The Mound Builders. New York: Franklin Watts, 1974.

Nancy Hanks of Wilderness Road. New York: Alfred A. Knopf, 1949; Duluth: Holy Cow! Press, 1997.

North Star Country. New York: Duell, Sloan, & Pearce, 1945; Lincoln: University of Nebraska Press, 1984; Minneapolis: University of Minnesota Press, 1998.

Ripening. New York: The Feminist Press, 1982, 1990.

Rites of Ancient Ripening. Minneapolis: Vanilla Press, 1975; Meridel LeSueur and David Tilsen, 1982.

The River Road: A Story of Abraham Lincoln. New York: Alfred A. Knopf, 1954; Duluth: Holy Cow! Press, 1991.

Salute to Spring. New York: International Publishers, 1940, 1977, 1981.

Song for My Time. Albuquerque: West End Press, 1977.

Sparrow Hawk. New York: Alfred A. Knopf, 1950; Duluth: Holy Cow! Press, 1987.

Winter Prairie Woman. Minneapolis: Minnesota Center for Book Arts, 1990; Minneapolis: Midwest Villages & Voices, 1991.

Women on the Breadlines. Albuquerque: West End Press, 1977, 1984.

Worker Writer. Albuquerque: West End Press, 1982.